The Zero Dollar millionaire

I0515023

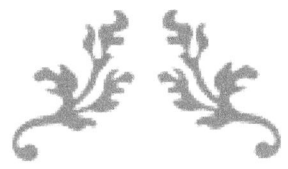

THE ZERO DOLLAR MILLIONAIRE

How to become rich on a Low-Income

JEFF ANTHONY

Copyright © 2024 *Jeff Anthony*

All rights reserved. No part of this book may be reproduced or used in any manner without the prior written permission of the copyright owner, except for the use of brief quotations in a book review.

TABLE OF CONTENTS

Introduction 6
The Journey Begins 6
   My Story: From Zero to Wealth 7
   Why This Book Can Change Your Life 11
Chapter 1. 13
The Millionaire Mindset 13
   Developing a Wealthy Mindset 14
   Overcoming Limiting Beliefs 16
   Visualizing Success and Setting Goals 18
Chapter 2. 21
Financial Literacy: Understanding Money 21
   The Basics of Money Management 22
   Assets vs. Liabilities: Knowing the Difference 25
   Budgeting for Success on a Low Income 27
Chapter 3. 31
Smart Saving Strategies 31
   The Importance of Saving Early 32
   Creative Ways to Save More 33
   Building an Emergency Fund 35

Chapter 4. 38

Earning More: Enhancing Your Income 38

    Side Hustles and Passive Income Streams 39

    Negotiating Raises and Promotions 41

    Leveraging Skills for Profit 43

Chapter 5. 46

Investing Wisely: Building Your Portfolio 46

    The Power of Compound Interest 47

    Introduction to Stocks, Bonds, and Real Estate 49

    Diversification: Protecting Your Investments 51

Chapter 6. 54

Real Estate: The Wealth Builder 54

    Why Real Estate is a Key to Wealth 55

    Finding Opportunities in the Property Market 57

    Renting vs. Owning: What Works for You 59

Chapter 7. 62

Business Ventures: Turning Ideas into Income 62

    Starting Your Own Business on a Budget 63

    Identifying Market Needs and Opportunities 65

Chapter 8. 70

Financial Roadblocks: Navigating Challenges 70

Common Financial Pitfalls to Avoid 71
Learning from Failures and Mistakes 73
Building Resilience and Staying Motivated............... 75

Chapter 9. 78

Mindful Spending: Aligning Purchases with Values ... 78

Conscious Consumerism: Spending with Purpose ... 79
Cutting Unnecessary Expenses.................................... 81
Living Below Your Means Without Sacrificing Joy . 83

Chapter 10. 86

Debt Management: Breaking Free from the Chains ... 86

Understanding Good vs. Bad Debt............................. 87
Strategies for Paying Off Debt Quickly 89
Staying Debt-Free for Life 91

Chapter 11. 94

Planning for the Future: Retirement and Beyond 94

Retirement Planning on a Low Income 95
The Power of Long-Term Thinking............................ 97
Leaving a Legacy for Future Generations 98

Chapter 12. 101

Living the Millionaire Lifestyle 101

Redefining What It Means to Be Wealthy................ 102

- Experiences Over Possessions: Finding True Happiness 104
- Giving Back: Using Wealth for Good 106

Chapter 13. 108

Becoming Financially Independent 108

- Achieving Financial Independence and Freedom ... 109
- The Steps to Becoming a Self-Made Millionaire 111
- Celebrating Your Success and Sharing Your Story 114

Conclusion: 116

Your Path to Wealth 116

- The Ongoing Pursuit of Growth and Knowledge ... 117
- Final Words of Encouragement 118

Bibliography 121

INTRODUCTION
THE JOURNEY BEGINS

"True wealth is not measured by how much money you have, but by the freedom to pursue your passions and the ability to make a positive impact on the lives of others."

This concept, which is based on the advice of numerous prosperous businesspeople, gets to the core of achieving financial success. The pursuit of freedom, stability, and contentment in life is the true meaning of wealth, which goes beyond a figure in a bank account.

Have you ever had dreams of a life in which your concerns about money don't hold you back? A life in which you are able to provide for your family, follow your passions, and give back to the community? You can achieve that dream. To begin this path, you must make the decision to alter your financial future.

MY STORY: FROM ZERO TO WEALTH

Allow me to take you back to Scranton, a little Pennsylvanian town where my journey started. I'm Jeff Anthony, and I was raised in a household that was never wealthy. Despite their arduous efforts, my parents' dream of financial security remained far off. I have a strong awareness for the worth of hard effort and a strong desire to end the cycle of scarcity because of my background.

I worked at any job I could find as a teenager, from delivering newspapers to mowing lawns. I soon realized how valuable every dollar was and how important it was to save and spend money carefully. These early teachings prepared me for success in the future.

A Humble Beginning

I had to make a crucial choice after high school: continue living a humble life in Scranton or take a risk and follow my goals. I went with option number two, moving to New York City with little more than a $100 bill and a luggage. I was resolved to forge a new path for myself, even though it was risky.

I was a waiter in a busy diner in New York while I went to community college. While it was a difficult period, I also started to get really interested in personal finance during that time. I watched instructional videos, read a ton of books, and tried to learn everything I could about investing and accumulating wealth.

I found a book about successful people's mindsets to be quite relatable. It showed me that creating wealth involves more than just getting money; it also involves making money work for you. I began implementing these ideas in my own life after having this paradigm-shifting realization.

Building Wealth from Scratch

Having gained some fresh insight, I started putting my meager funds into stocks. Though it wasn't much, it was a beginning. I gained knowledge about the value of perseverance and compound interest. My confidence increased along with my investments.

Acquiring a tiny rental property in an area that was undergoing development was my first major real estate venture. Even though it was a difficult undertaking, I saw possibility where others saw danger. This turned out to be one of my best choices because it set the stage for my financial success in the future.

My entrepreneurial drive inspired me and a friend to Co-found a digital marketing agency. We began modestly, operating out of a small Brooklyn flat. Our organization expanded quickly as a result of our commitment and enthusiasm for fostering the success of small enterprises. We quickly recruited a strong staff, grew our clientele, and relocated to a Manhattan office.

I became financially successful by being persistent, working hard, and making wise decisions. I didn't become a millionaire overnight; rather, I did it by taking methodical steps and picking up lessons from every setback.

I live with my family in Austin, Texas, these days. My journey from poverty to fortune has changed me profoundly and given me priceless insights about life, money, and resiliency.

WHY THIS BOOK CAN CHANGE YOUR LIFE

Have you ever had the impression that your finances are stagnating and you're just treading water? This is how a lot of people feel, but it doesn't have to be your reality. By changing your perspective and putting tried-and-true methods into practice, you can alter your financial destiny.

This is about obtaining financial freedom, not just about hoarding wealth. Imagine leading a life in which your finances are managed by you rather than the other way around. You may support your family, follow your passions, and get involved in issues that are important to you.

Here are some questions to consider:

- What would it mean for you to achieve financial independence and break free from the cycle of debt?

- How would your life change if you had the resources to support your loved ones and positively impact your community?
- Are you ready to take charge of your financial destiny and create a future filled with possibilities?

Anyone who is prepared to put in the necessary effort and learn is able to achieve financial success; it is not only a privilege for a select few. This book provides guidance on how to reach your full potential and improve your financial situation.

You have the ability to achieve financial success; all it takes is choosing to take charge of your life. You have the ability to alter your situation, and now is the time to start that process.

CHAPTER 1. THE MILLIONAIRE MINDSET

"Whether you think you can, or you think you can't—you're right."

— Henry Ford

The most effective tool you have in your quest to become a millionaire is your mind. How far you can go will depend on how you view money, success, and your own potential. A lot of people think that luck plays a role in being affluent, but in reality, mentality plays a major role. The first step to financial freedom is to cultivate a billionaire mindset, as your thoughts create your reality.

DEVELOPING A WEALTHY MINDSET

The wealthy think differently. They see the world through a lens of opportunity, not scarcity. This difference in perspective is what separates those who accumulate wealth from those who struggle financially.

One of the most important lessons I learned on my journey to wealth is that money is not the root of all evil; it's a tool—a tool that can be used to create freedom, security, and positive change. People with a wealthy mindset understand that money itself is neutral. It's how you use it that matters.

Consider this: How do you view money? Do you see it as something to be hoarded and feared, or do you see it as a means to achieve your goals and help others? If you want to become wealthy, you must begin to see money as an ally, not an enemy.

I remember when I first started my journey. I was living in New York City, working long hours as a waiter, and barely making ends meet. I was frustrated and often questioned whether I would ever achieve financial success. But then, I began to shift my thinking. Instead of focusing on what I didn't have, I started to focus on what I could create. I began to see opportunities where others saw obstacles. This shift in mindset was the turning point for me.

You see, your thoughts create your reality. If you believe that wealth is unattainable, it will be. But if you believe that you have the power to create wealth, you will start to see opportunities everywhere. Developing a wealthy mindset is about shifting your focus from limitations to possibilities. It's about believing that you deserve financial success and that you have the power to achieve it.

OVERCOMING LIMITING BELIEFS

Limiting attitudes regarding money keep a lot of people back. These are the kinds of beliefs and mindsets that trap you in a never-ending cycle of financial hardship. Commonly held limiting beliefs include the ideas that "money is hard to come by," "I'm not good with money," or "I don't deserve to be rich." These beliefs are just stories we tell ourselves; they are not truths.

Being conscious of limiting ideas is the first step towards conquering them. Take note of your thoughts and your language when discussing money to begin with. Are there phrases like "I can't afford that" or "I'll never be able to save enough" that you find yourself saying? These indicate the presence of limiting ideas and require attention.

I overcame my own limiting beliefs by substituting positive affirmations for my negative ideas. For instance, I might ask, "How can I afford that?" as opposed to, "I can't afford that." The emphasis is shifted from limitation to opportunity by this straightforward linguistic modification.

Assembling a supportive network around oneself is another effective strategy. Spend time with folks who manage their money well, read books, and tune in to podcasts. It gets easier to adjust your attitudes about riches the more positive messages about it you are exposed to.

I had doubts at times when I was developing my digital marketing company. There were moments when I doubted my ability to achieve. However, I overcame those misgivings by reminding myself that success was achievable and by not allowing myself to be limited by my beliefs. It wasn't simple, but I was able to persevere and accomplish my objectives by persistently confronting those unfavorable thoughts.

Recall that you can relearn whatever you have learned, including your beliefs about money. Your story can be written over by you.

VISUALIZING SUCCESS AND SETTING GOALS

Successful people use visualization as a great tool to accomplish their objectives. Your mind and body can follow a mental blueprint you build when you visualize your desired goal clearly. This is a technique that has been shown to improve motivation, focus, and performance—it's not just wishful thinking.

Shut your eyes for a moment and visualize the kind of life you wish to have. Imagine living in your ideal house, traveling in your ideal vehicle, and working at a job you enjoy every day. What is the sensation? How would you describe your day? Your success will seem more genuine in your imagination the more vividly you can picture it.

I used to see the life I wanted to lead a lot when I was fighting to make ends meet in that tiny Brooklyn apartment. I pictured myself owning a lovely home, supporting my family, and operating a profitable business. Even at difficult moments, I was able to stay motivated and focused because to these images.

But setting specific, attainable goals is just as important as using visualization alone. Those who are successful plan instead of just dreaming. Establishing objectives helps you track your progress and provides you with a defined route to follow.

To begin, put your financial objectives in paper. Give details. Rather than stating your wish to be wealthy, make a goal such as "I want to buy my first rental property within two years" or "I want to save $10,000 in the next year." Divide these objectives into more achievable segments, and assign due dates to each one.

My initial investment objective was to save $1,000 for my first stock buy. Although it wasn't much, it was a start. I saved a little sum of money every week, and in a few of months, I had accomplished my objective. My quest to prosperity was started by that initial investment.

As you accomplish your objectives, make new ones. Continue challenging yourself to go farther and accomplish more. Recall that success is a journey rather than a destination. Reaching your goals takes you one step closer to living the life you've always desired.

CHAPTER 2.
FINANCIAL LITERACY: UNDERSTANDING MONEY

"The single most powerful asset we all have is our mind. If it is trained well, it can create enormous wealth."

— Robert Kiyosaki

Gaining financial stability is essential to accumulating wealth. The secret to financial success, according to popular belief, is not more money but rather effective use of the money you already have. Understanding how money works, how to make it work for you, and how to avoid typical errors that can leave you stuck in a never-ending cycle of financial difficulty are all part of financial literacy.

THE BASICS OF MONEY MANAGEMENT

Effective money management is the cornerstone on which all wealth is constructed. Even a substantial salary can be squandered without effective management. While some people with modest earnings manage to accumulate substantial wealth, I've seen people with six-figure wages living paycheck to paycheck. Their methods of managing their finances varies.

Knowing what your income and expenses are is the first step to being an expert money manager. You must be fully aware of the amount of money coming in and going out. Although it may seem easy, a lot of people don't monitor their expenditures. They occasionally use credit cards to make small purchases, and before they realize it, they are in debt.

When I initially began working, I meticulously tracked every dollar I made and spent. Even though I didn't have a lot of money, I respected what I did have. I was able to find areas where I could make savings and reduce back thanks to this technique. I came to see that little, pointless expenses added up rapidly and that by cutting them out, I could allocate more funds to my objectives.

Prioritize saving if you want to handle your finances well. The wealthy are aware that saving money is about building a financial cushion that enables you to seize opportunities as they present themselves, not just setting money aside for a rainy day. Prioritize your own needs by allocating a portion of your earnings for savings before making any other purchases. Over time, it accumulates, even if it's only a little sum.

Knowing interest rates is also essential to managing money, especially when it comes to debt. Similar to credit card debt, high-interest debt has the potential to rapidly get out of control if improperly managed. High-interest debt must be paid off as soon as possible because the interest may wind up costing you much more than the original purchase. Conversely, knowing how compound interest works might help you accumulate more wealth. Investing results in the accumulation of interest on your money, which eventually generates interest of its own, starting a chain reaction that can result in significant growth.

I still recall the day I purchased my first rental home. I took into account more than just the purchase price; I also looked at the possibility for rental income, the property taxes, and the interest rate on the mortgage. To make sure the property would be a wise investment and not a financial burden, I did the math. You must engage in this kind of thorough financial planning if you hope to accumulate and maintain money.

ASSETS VS. LIABILITIES: KNOWING THE DIFFERENCE

Knowing the distinction between assets and liabilities is one of the most crucial financial literacy courses. Liabilities take money out of your pocket, whereas assets put money in it. Although this may sound simple, a lot of people find it difficult to understand since they mistakenly identify liabilities as assets.

A house, for instance, is frequently regarded as an asset. But, if you have a mortgage and your home isn't profitable, then it becomes a liability. You are responsible for covering the costs of upkeep, insurance, property taxes, and the mortgage out of your own cash. Conversely, an asset is something that generates revenue, like a business, dividend-paying stocks, or a rental property.

My perspective on finances was altered by realizing this distinction. I used to dream of having a large house and an expensive car. But I came to understand that although these were wonderful to have, they wouldn't make me wealthy. Rather, I concentrated on obtaining assets—items that would produce revenue and increase in value over time.

A little stock portfolio was among my initial possessions. Even though I didn't have much money to invest at the time, I did purchase a small number of shares in businesses I supported. Those stocks increased in value over time, and a few of them even started to pay dividends. I had an epiphany when I realized that I was earning money without having to work for it. I was able to reinvest and increase my fortune even more because to this passive income.

However, I took care to limit my responsibilities. Rather than financing a new car, I drove an older, paid-off one. Before I was financially ready, I opted to rent a modest apartment rather than purchase a house. I was able to focus on increasing my assets and eventually achieved financial freedom by reducing my responsibilities.

BUDGETING FOR SUCCESS ON A LOW INCOME

Although it's sometimes perceived as a limiting practice, budgeting is actually a tool that helps you gain financial control. All it is, a budget is a strategy for how much money you will spend and save. It enables you to set spending priorities, stay out of debt, and make sure you're setting aside enough money for the future.

Making a budget is much more important if you have a limited income. Make sure your money is working as hard as you are because every dollar matters. Listing all of your sources of income and fixed costs, including rent, utilities, and groceries, is the first step in making a budget. Next, consider your discretionary spending, which includes items like shopping, entertainment, and eating out. Here's where you'll frequently find places to make savings.

I had to practice extreme financial discipline when I was living on a restricted budget in New York City. I was unable to frequently eat out or purchase unnecessary items. However, I also didn't want to feel poor, so I looked for methods to have fun without going over budget. For instance, I would cook at home and host friends instead of dining at pricey establishments. I watched free shows online or checked out movies from the library rather of paying for cable.

Being flexible and practical when creating a budget is essential for those with modest incomes. Establish definite financial objectives, such as putting money aside for an emergency fund or buying your first asset, and set aside money for them each month. Make sure you're remaining within your budget by keeping track of your expenditures, but don't be too hard on yourself if you periodically overspend. Maintaining forward motion is crucial.

Additionally, budgeting helps you stay out of the lifestyle inflation trap. The temptation to spend more on pleasures increases as your income rises. However, you will never succeed financially if you raise your expenses in tandem with increases in income. Instead, make an effort to stick to your budget even if your income rises, and utilize the excess cash for investments, debt repayment, or savings for future objectives.

Although it may not sound glamorous, one of the most effective tools in your financial toolbox is budgeting. No matter how little money you make, it empowers you to make informed financial decisions and guarantees that you're always taking steps toward your financial objectives.

CHAPTER 3. SMART SAVING STRATEGIES

"Do not wait; the time will never be 'just right.' Start where you stand, and work with whatever tools you may have at your command."

— Napoleon Hill

The foundation of sound financial management is saving money. It is a habit that ought to be developed early and continuously because it is the cornerstone around which riches is constructed. But saving is about more than just setting aside a percentage of your income—it's about saving with purpose. Discipline, imagination, and a long-term outlook are necessary for wise saving. Here's how you can turn saving into a task.

THE IMPORTANCE OF SAVING EARLY

One of the most potent allies on the path to financial independence is time. Your money has more time to develop if you start saving early. This isn't just about saving money; it's also about taking advantage of compound interest, which allows savings to grow into earnings, which in turn generate even more earnings. Similar to planting a tree, it will bear fruit sooner if you do it sooner.

I'll give you an example from my personal experience. I wasn't wealthy when I initially started working. Nonetheless, I prioritized saving a little portion of my monthly salary since I understood how important it is to do so. At first, it wasn't much, but as time passed, I started to notice compounding's effects. Those little sums added up.

and as I kept up my regular saving, my savings started to grow on their own.

It's like having an advantage when saving early in a race. It becomes more difficult for anyone—or any financial challenge—to catch up the further ahead you go. Start saving right away, even if it's just a small amount. Don't wait until you feel like you have enough or until you are making more money. No matter how little you start with, the important thing is to keep adding to it.

CREATIVE WAYS TO SAVE MORE

It's not necessary to give up everything you enjoy in order to save money. Actually, some of the most effective ways to save money are entertaining and innovative. It's about figuring out how to save costs without compromising your standard of living.

One strategy that I found most successful was automating my savings. I never even noticed the money in my bank account because I had automated transfers to my savings account set up for when I got paid. It made saving simple and supported my consistency.

Utilizing cashback and rewards programs is a another tactic. It would be wise to make a profit if you are already planning to spend money. These little benefits, such as cashback on purchases from credit cards or retailer loyalty programs, can mount up over time.

I also discovered methods to cut costs by using creativity in my purchases. For instance, I started purchasing goods in bulk from bargain retailers when I went grocery shopping. Additionally, I discovered that cooking at home more frequently not only helped me save money but also enhanced my health. Rather than shelling out cash for pricey club subscriptions, I worked out at home using free online fitness plans. I was able to save more without feeling deprived thanks to these minor adjustments.

I named this clever savings method "The 30-Day Rule," and it was one of my favorites. I would wait 30 days before making a purchase if I wanted to acquire something that wasn't necessary. I frequently came to the conclusion that I didn't actually need the item by the time the 30-day period was up. I was able to control my spending and maintain a larger balance in my savings account as a result.

BUILDING AN EMERGENCY FUND

Because life is unpredictable, it is essential to have an emergency fund. This is the money you have set aside especially for unforeseen costs, such as auto repairs, medical bills, or losing your job. When something unexpected happens in life, an emergency fund serves as a safety net to keep you out of debt.

Building up my emergency money was top priority for me when I first started out. I began modest, trying to save just enough to pay for my bills for a month. After I accomplished that target, I kept saving until I had enough money to pay for three or six months' worth of expenses. I felt more at ease knowing that I wouldn't have to rely on loans or credit cards in case something unforeseen occurred.

Establishing an emergency fund takes discipline, but the work is worthwhile. Setting it as a top priority is crucial. Decide on a precise objective, like saving $1,000, and make steady progress toward it. After achieving that objective, make a new one. Continue developing until you have enough cushion to meet your daily expenses for a few months.

Your emergency cash should be kept in a different, readily accessible account, such a savings account. In this manner, the funds are accessible when needed, but accessing them for non-emergencies is more difficult. Recall that an emergency fund should only be used for actual emergencies—not for needs or wishes.

Having an emergency fund gives you peace of mind in addition to financial stability. It makes life less stressful to take measured chances, chase opportunities, and know that you have a safety net in place. It's one of the most crucial components of a wise saving plan, and everyone should prioritize it, regardless of wealth.

CHAPTER 4. EARNING MORE: ENHANCING YOUR INCOME

"The best investment you can make is in yourself."

— Warren Buffett

One of the best methods to hasten your path to financial independence is to raise your income. Budgeting and saving are important, but eventually earning more money is the only way to go forward significantly. The important thing is to take charge of your financial future by actively looking for ways to increase your income, whether it is through side gigs, passive income streams, skill-based entrepreneurship, or salary negotiation.

SIDE HUSTLES AND PASSIVE INCOME STREAMS

It is dangerous to depend only on one source of income in the modern world. Living expenses are constantly increasing, and work stability is never assured. Side projects and passive income sources are useful in this situation. Any task you do outside of your normal employment to earn extra money is referred to as a side hustle, whereas passive income is money made with little to no ongoing effort.

I understood early on that a 9–5 work wouldn't be enough to bring me where I wanted to go financially. I thus started looking into secondary projects. I experimented with everything, including online sales and freelance work. While some of my endeavors proved to be more prosperous than others, what mattered most was that I was expanding my sources of income and picking up new abilities in the process.

Finding ways to transform your passions and skills into profit is one of the most important lessons I've learned about side hustles. It's not just about generating extra money. If you're skilled in graphic design, for instance, you might market your freelance skills on sites like Upwork or Fiverr. If you're a talented writer, you might want to write an ebook or launch a blog. These side projects not only help you supplement your income but also free up time for you to work on projects you enjoy.

On the other side, passive income enables you to make money even while you're not working. This could involve making dividend-paying stock investments, renting out real estate, or developing a long-term selling product like an online course or digital download. The great thing about passive income is that it grows steadily over time, giving you the opportunity to gradually replace your active income with sources of revenue that need little upkeep.

Buying assets that paid dividends was one of my earliest attempts at generating passive income. Even though I didn't have much money at first, I regularly put some of my profits into these companies. My dividends increased over time, and I reinvested them to purchase additional shares. Although it wasn't a get-rich-quick plan, it was a consistent and trustworthy method of accumulating riches.

NEGOTIATING RAISES AND PROMOTIONS

The ability to bargain for promotions and raises is another essential to increasing your revenue. A lot of people don't realize how powerful it is to just ask for what they deserve. You should be paid appropriately if you're skilled at what you do and can demonstrate it with your accomplishments.

I was afraid to request a raise in the beginning of my career. I didn't want to come out as ungrateful or greedy. But later on, I understood that no one else would stand up for me if I didn't. I therefore began looking into market prices for my role and became ready to make a case for my supervisor. I emphasized my achievements, the value I added to the business, and the fact that I had taken on more responsibility.

When the time came, I made a bold and fact-based request for a raise. My employer surprised me by agreeing, and I was given a sizable raise. I learned from this experience that asking for what you deserve and believing in your own value are essential for achieving financial success. It's not always the case that employers will give you a raise or promotion; occasionally, you will need to go it alone and bargain for it.

However, negotiating entails more than just demanding more money. It all comes down to realizing your worth and putting yourself in a situation where you become invaluable. This entails developing your abilities on a constant basis, accepting new challenges, and demonstrating that you're not just completing your work but exceeding expectations. By doing this, you make a compelling argument for why you should be given more.

LEVERAGING SKILLS FOR PROFIT

Using the skills you already possess is one of the best methods to increase your income. All people possess special talents and abilities, but not all people know how to make money with those skills. Finding methods to get money from what you're good at is the key.

For example, I was aware that I had a knack for real estate, but I didn't grow up learning how to purchase and sell real estate. I began by reading as much as I could about the market, going to seminars, and building relationships with knowledgeable investors. I gained a thorough grasp of real estate over time, and I started using that expertise to my advantage by purchasing homes at a discount and reselling them for a profit.

However, using your abilities doesn't always entail launching a new company. There are instances when it comes to figuring out how to improve your existing position or sector. If you work as an accountant, for instance, you may provide tax preparation services on the side. If you work as an educator, you can design online courses or tutor students. Using your existing knowledge to create new revenue sources is the aim.

Leveraging your abilities has several benefits, not the least of which is that it frequently takes little to no upfront investment. All you're doing is converting your existing skill set into a revenue stream. Your abilities also become more valuable the more you hone and develop them, which enables you to charge more and draw in better chances.

Working more intelligently rather than merely harder is the key to increasing your revenue. You can establish several routes to financial success by using your skills, negotiating for what you're worth, and diversifying your sources of income. Although it's not always simple, the benefits are well worth the work.

CHAPTER 5. INVESTING WISELY: BUILDING YOUR PORTFOLIO

"An investment in knowledge pays the best interest."

— Benjamin Franklin

The secret to gradually increasing your wealth is investing. Saving money is important, but it's just the beginning. You must make your money work for you in order to genuinely accumulate riches. This entails allocating your money to investments with the potential to increase in value over time and produce returns that will enable you to meet your financial objectives. But making smart investments calls for understanding, perseverance, and a well-thought-out plan. This chapter will introduce you to a variety of investing options, go over the power of compound interest, and go over the significance of diversification in safeguarding your wealth.

THE POWER OF COMPOUND INTEREST

One of the most potent forces in the financial world is compound interest. It's the idea of receiving interest on interest that accrues over time in addition to your initial investment. Your money increases in value the longer it is invested because interest compounded annually.

Permit me to give you an example from my experience. I didn't have much money to invest in the market when I initially started. However, I was aware that consistency and an early start were essential to accumulating wealth. I started by making little investments in a basic savings account that offered a low interest return. I eventually switched to higher-yielding investments like bonds and equities.

Despite my modest beginning investments, the magic of compound interest allowed my fortune to increase dramatically over time. For example, if you invest $1,000 at a 5% annual interest rate, you will receive approximately $1,628 after ten years. However, that money increases to almost $2,653 if you leave it invested for 20 years. Compound interest works like magic when you use time as your biggest ally.

Starting early and maintaining consistency in your investments are essential to maximizing the power of compound interest. Make the investment, even if it's just a tiny amount each month. Your wealth will increase over time when you start early since your money will have more time to grow.

INTRODUCTION TO STOCKS, BONDS, AND REAL ESTATE

Investing is more than just putting money in a savings account—it's also about selecting the best investments to increase your wealth. The three most popular investment categories are real estate, bonds, and stocks. Each has advantages and disadvantages of its own, and developing a solid portfolio requires an awareness of the fundamentals of each.

Stocks represent ownership in a company. Purchasing shares entitles you to a tiny portion of the company. Your stock value rises in tandem with the company's growth and profitability, and you stand to win from both dividends and capital gains. Although stocks are known for their ability to yield large profits, there is a greater risk associated with them. Stock prices are subject to market fluctuations, so it's critical to conduct due diligence and choose investments in businesses with solid fundamentals.

Bonds are essentially loans that you give to a company or government. You receive your initial investment back when the bond matures, and they pay you interest over a certain length of time in exchange. Because they have a fixed income and are less volatile than stocks, bonds are often thought to be safer than equities. They do, however, also provide lesser rewards. Bonds are a fantastic choice for investors who want greater stability or for those who are getting close to retirement and want to protect their capital.

Real estate is another powerful investment tool. Purchasing real estate entails investing in a tangible asset that has the potential to yield income through either rental income or appreciation over time. Many investors like real estate because it has the ability to yield both consistent income flow and long-term gain. However, real estate has its own set of hazards, including market swings and property upkeep fees, and demands a sizable upfront investment.

I didn't have enough money when I first started investing in real estate to buy a property outright. I thus painstakingly saved money and eventually used a mortgage to buy my first rental property. The mortgage payments were eventually paid off by the rental revenue, and the property's value increased. One of the pillars of my fortune today is that first investment.

DIVERSIFICATION: PROTECTING YOUR INVESTMENTS

Diversification is among the most crucial financial concepts. This entails distributing your assets over various asset classes (e.g., stocks, bonds, and real estate) as well as within those classes (e.g., investing in various industries or geographical areas). By spreading your bets, you should be able to lower your risk.

Your assets are shielded from the volatility of any one asset by diversification. Your portfolio may be balanced if, for instance, the stock market declines but your bonds or real estate investments hold steady. Conversely, you're more susceptible to market swings if you solely invest in one class of asset, like equities.

I made sure to diversify early in my personal portfolio. I made a variety of investments in bonds with varied maturities, real estate in various places, and stocks from various businesses. Because of my portfolio's diversification, I was able to withstand market fluctuations and maintain steady growth over time.

However, diversity also aims to maximize profits in addition to risk management. You can improve your chances of making money from various sources by diversifying your investments because different asset classes perform well at different periods. It all comes down to creating a portfolio that can expand and withstand fluctuations in the market.

Developing a diverse portfolio calls for careful planning. First, determine your financial objectives and risk tolerance. After that, distribute your investments appropriately. Recall that the objective is to create a portfolio that can develop steadily over time, not only to amass assets.

CHAPTER 6.
REAL ESTATE: THE WEALTH BUILDER

"Ninety percent of all millionaires become so through owning real estate."

— Andrew Carnegie

One of the most dependable and effective methods for accumulating wealth is real estate, which has been acknowledged for a long time. When done properly, this investment can yield not only cash gains but also a feeling of stability and security. This chapter will discuss the benefits of owning versus renting, the reasons real estate is essential to wealth, and how to identify possibilities in the real estate market.

WHY REAL ESTATE IS A KEY TO WEALTH

The special benefit of real estate is that it may be a source of income in addition to being a tangible asset. Real estate is something you can see, touch, and improve, as opposed to stocks and bonds, which are simply represented on paper. It has a certain solidity and security that other investments can't always provide because of its tangible form.

One of the biggest advantages of real estate is **leverage**. When buying real estate, you have the option to use borrowed funds—a mortgage—to purchase an asset that is far more valuable than what you paid up-front. For instance, you could buy a $200,000 house with a $20,000 down payment. You receive appreciation on the entire worth of the property when its value rises, not just the amount of your down payment. One of the ways that real estate investing can result in substantial riches is the capacity to leverage your funds.

Furthermore, real estate offers other revenue streams. Rent payments are a passive source of revenue if you own rental properties. Your net worth grows as you pay off your mortgage over time because you have more equity in the house. Moreover, real estate frequently increases in value over time, giving you substantial gains when you want to sell.

I'll give you a personal illustration. I initially invested in real estate by purchasing a modest duplex in a developing area. I rented out one apartment while I resided in the other. I was able to live rent-free while my house appreciated in value because the rental revenue more than paid my mortgage. I made a big profit on the sale of the property after a few years, and I invested the money in other properties. Using one property as leverage to buy more is a traditional real estate wealth-building tactic.

FINDING OPPORTUNITIES IN THE PROPERTY MARKET

Not all real estate markets are made equal. The location, timing, and state of the market can all have a significant impact on opportunities. Finding profitable real estate investments requires careful study and a calculated approach.

Recognize the local market first. Which property values are trending? Is the population of the area dwindling or is it growing? Exist any upcoming construction projects or infrastructural initiatives that might raise property values in the future? Each of these elements has the potential to affect how profitable a real estate investment is.

Seek out regions that are about to expand. The greatest real estate chances are frequently located in areas that are just beginning to gain popularity.

Although the initial cost of real estate in these places may be lower, as the area grows and more people move there, the value of real estate can increase dramatically. Purchasing real estate in emerging communities has always been successful for me since it allowed me to get in before prices soared.

The state of the property is another crucial factor. Sometimes, if you're prepared to put in the work, a property that requires some maintenance might be a terrific investment. You can raise the value of a fixer-upper and earn a sizable profit when you sell or rent it out by buying it for less money and making changes.

It's also critical to take cash flow potential into account. Consider the local rental market while assessing a rental property. How much do comparable houses rent for? Will your mortgage, taxes, and maintenance expenses be paid for by the rental income? A good investment is a property that generates positive cash flow right away.

RENTING VS. OWNING: WHAT WORKS FOR YOU

Whether to buy or rent is one of the biggest financial decisions you will have to make. Each option has advantages, and the best one for you will rely on your lifestyle, long-term objectives, and financial condition.

Owning a home is often seen as the American Dream, and for good reason. Being a homeowner gives you the opportunity to accumulate equity over time, take advantage of property appreciation, and possess a place of your own. Your monthly mortgage payment goes toward equity in your home instead of a landlord when you own it. Your property increases in value as you pay down your mortgage over time, giving you greater equity that you can use to make other investments or leave to your descendants.

But house ownership also entails hazards and duties. You bear the responsibility for upkeep, fixes, real estate taxes, and homeowner's insurance. Furthermore, the market might affect the value of your house, and selling a house can take time if you need to relocate urgently.

On the other hand, **renting** offers flexibility and lower upfront costs. If you want to keep your money flexible for other investments or if you're not ready to settle down in one location, renting can be a better option. Renters are not immediately impacted by a downturn in the housing market and are not obligated to maintain or repair the property.

During my early years, I saved money for my first real estate investment by renting a small apartment. I was able to invest in other chances and save money by renting instead of having to worry about paying for a house. I started building my real estate portfolio and bought my first property when I had enough saved and the ideal chance presented itself.

Generally speaking, buying real estate is a preferable alternative for anyone hoping to increase their wealth through it. Before choosing, it's crucial to evaluate your lifestyle and financial circumstances. Until you're financially ready to buy, renting could be the best option in some circumstances. The secret is to make decisions based on your long-term objectives and to have a well-defined plan.

CHAPTER 7.
BUSINESS VENTURES: TURNING IDEAS INTO INCOME

"The way to get started is to quit talking and begin doing."

— **Walt Disney**

Creating a successful business out of an idea is one of the most effective methods to make money. Although the path from idea to successful business endeavor is difficult, anyone can turn their ideas into a reliable source of revenue with perseverance, ingenuity, and astute planning. This chapter will walk you through the steps of creating a budget-friendly business plan, determining market possibilities and needs, and growing your company.

STARTING YOUR OWN BUSINESS ON A BUDGET

Funding is not a major barrier to business startup. All it took for many prosperous business owners to get started was a solid concept and the will to see it through to completion. Using your limited resources strategically and creatively is the key.

Clearly defining your company idea is the first stage. Which goods or services do you provide? What issue does it resolve? Your target market is who? By providing answers to these questions, you'll have a strong basis on which to grow.

I didn't have a lot of money to put in a business when I initially started out, but I was passionate about assisting people in building wealth and saving money. Thus, while continuing to work my full-time job, I began to provide financial advising services on the side. All I needed for my early expenses was a website, a few business cards, and a lot of work. I conducted business using free internet tools while meeting with clients in coffee cafes. I gradually increased my services and clientele by progressively investing my money back into the company as my clientele developed.

Reduce your overhead expenditures if you want to launch your firm on a shoestring. When possible, use materials and technologies that are free or inexpensive. Consider working from home or using a co-working space as an alternative to renting an office. Consider working with freelancers or outsourcing jobs rather than immediately hiring staff. The objective is to keep costs to a minimum as you test your concept and begin to make money.

Making a minimal viable product is another crucial step (MVP). This is your most basic offering to the market for your product or service. It only needs to fulfill a need or address an issue; perfection is not required. You may launch your firm rapidly, get client feedback, and make adjustments without having to invest a large sum of money up front by starting with an MVP.

IDENTIFYING MARKET NEEDS AND OPPORTUNITIES

Every prosperous company begins by determining a market need. Entrepreneurship projects that solve an issue or satisfy an unmet demand tend to be the most successful. You must be perceptive, pay attention to what potential clients have to say, and be open to changing your idea to suit the needs and opportunities of the market in order to spot opportunities.

Investigate your market and industry first. Which trends are prevalent right now? What requests do customers have? Which are the holes in the market that you could address? The finest business ideas occasionally originate from personal frustrations or experiences. If you've ever yearned for a good or service that doesn't exist yet, for instance, there might be other people who share your sentiments.

After determining whether there may be a market demand, test your hypothesis by speaking with possible clients. Get their opinion on the idea of your product or service. Would they purchase it? To what extent would they be prepared to pay? Which qualities or advantages mean the most to them? You may improve your concept and make sure there is a market for what you're giving with the help of this feedback.

From personal experience, I found that a lot of people desired to participate in real estate but had the funds to purchase a home on their own. I created a real estate investing organization so that people could pool their funds and buy real estate together after noticing this gap in the market. This made it possible for those with little money to invest in real estate, and the group's combined purchasing power increased the chances of earning a profit.

SCALING YOUR BUSINESS FOR GROWTH

Scaling your firm for growth is the next issue when it is operational. Scaling entails growing your company to accommodate more clients, boost sales, and optimize earnings. It's all about maximizing what is currently effective.

Automation and delegating are two of the best strategies for growing a company. As your company expands, you won't be able to handle everything in-house. Your time can be better spent concentrating on strategic growth efforts by automating monotonous work and assigning duties to others. For instance, you can assign administrative responsibilities to a virtual assistant or use email marketing solutions to automate customer interactions.

To reach a wider audience, scaling also means reaching out farther. This could entail expanding into new markets, introducing new goods or services, or opening new sites. But it's crucial to scale carefully and gradually. Failure might result from expanding too quickly without the infrastructure or resources needed. Make sure you have a strong base and a well-defined growth management strategy before scaling.

During my journey, I discovered that forming alliances was essential to growing my company. I expanded my offers and reached new markets by collaborating with companies that provided complimentary services, all without incurring a large increase in expenses. For instance, I collaborated with a nearby bank to provide their clients with financial planning seminars. This collaboration increased my reputation in the neighborhood and brought in new business.

A further aspect of scaling is making ongoing improvements to your good or service in response to user input. Expectations from customers will rise as your business expands. Maintain a relationship with your clients, pay attention to their demands, and be prepared to adapt in order to satisfy them. Long-term growth depends on maintaining client happiness and loyalty, which can only be achieved by consistently improving and adapting.

CHAPTER 8. FINANCIAL ROADBLOCKS: NAVIGATING CHALLENGES

"Success is not final, failure is not fatal: It is the courage to continue that counts."

— Winston Churchill

The path to financial success is paved with obstacles. Every route to riches has its share of barriers along the way—times when the going gets tough and the challenges seem insurmountable. It's not the lack of obstacles but rather the ability to overcome them that makes the difference between people who reach their financial objectives and those who don't. This chapter focuses on developing the resilience required to maintain motivation in the face of adversity, learning from mistakes, and recognizing frequent financial hazards.

COMMON FINANCIAL PITFALLS TO AVOID

Falling into typical financial mistakes is one of the biggest obstacles to achieving financial success. If you're not careful, these are the blunders that can impede your advancement and cause you to regress. The good news is that, with the correct information and attitude, most of these mistakes can be avoided.

The most frequent trap is the inflation of lifestyle. It's easy to start overspending on comforts and frills when your income rises. However, regardless of your salary level, you will always find yourself in the same financial situation if your spending increase at the same rate as your income. To prevent this, continue your previous spending patterns from when you were making less money, and invest the extra money rather than squandering it.

A typical mistake is accruing excessive debt. When handled properly, debt can be a helpful tool, but if it is not controlled, it can become a financial trap. Similar to credit card debt, high-interest debt can easily get out of hand and reduce your income. If you're not careful, you can end yourself working simply to make ends meet and having little money left over for investments or savings. The secret is to stay out of debt and pay off any high-interest loans as soon as you can.

Making poor financial plans is another mistake that might prevent you from moving forward. It's simple to slip off course and lose sight of your financial objectives when you don't have a clear plan. This is the reason it's crucial to create a budget, set financial objectives, and periodically assess your finances. A carefully considered financial plan serves as a guide, assisting you in reaching your objectives and preventing roadblocks.

LEARNING FROM FAILURES AND MISTAKES

Any journey, including the path to financial success, will always include failure. The secret is to learn from failure instead of being afraid of it. Every error you make presents an opportunity to grow as a person and to make future decisions with a more refined approach.

I made several costly errors in my early real estate investing endeavors. Due to the low price, I purchased a property in a neighborhood whose value was dropping. I lost money since I had to sell it for less because I hadn't done enough research. It was a difficult lesson, but it made me realize how important it is to do extensive study before acting on bargains that appear too good to refuse after taking all the factors into account.

I learned from that setback rather than allowing it to depress me. I improved my investment plan, talked to more seasoned investors for assistance, and did more in-depth research on the real estate market. My next investments were far more profitable as a result. The most important thing to take away from this is that failure is merely a stepping stone. Giving up is the only true failure.

You will make mistakes and experience setbacks on your financial journey. Certain investments might not yield the anticipated returns, and certain prospects might not materialize. When this occurs, stand back and consider what went wrong. What can you take away from the encounter? How can you use that knowledge to inform your choices going forward? You develop into a more astute and resilient investor by taking lessons from your mistakes and setbacks.

BUILDING RESILIENCE AND STAYING MOTIVATED

Resilience is the capacity to pick oneself up after failures and carry on when things are difficult. It's an essential quality for anyone hoping to succeed financially because being rich is rarely an easy path. There will inevitably be periods of delayed progress, unforeseen costs, and market downturns. Resilience is what will get you through these times.

Having a solid why—a distinct understanding of why you're pursuing financial success—is the first step towards developing resilience. Your why is what propels you ahead, whether it's to support your family, become financially independent, or leave a legacy. Remind yourself of your initial motivation for embarking on this adventure whenever you encounter difficulties.

Positivity is another essential component of resilience building. Pay more attention to the strides you've achieved than the challenges you still face. Appreciate the little things in life and let them inspire you to keep going. Be in the company of uplifting people, including mentors, encouraging friends, or motivational literature. These motivational sources can support your motivation when things get tough.

During the 2008 financial crisis, I encountered one of the most significant obstacles in my financial journey. Like many others, I experienced a rough period both financially and emotionally when I watched the value of my investments drop. But I persisted rather than giving up and losing money on my investments. I reminded myself of the cycles in the markets and my long-term objectives. I bought cheap assets during the slump, and my investments eventually outperformed the market's recovery.

Taking care of oneself—both physically and mentally—is another aspect of resilience. If you're not careful, stress and burnout might ruin your financial objectives. Make time for hobbies, physical activity, and quality time with loved ones—things that help you rejuvenate. Taking care of your health guarantees that you will have the stamina and determination to go beyond obstacles and continue working toward your financial objectives.

CHAPTER 9. MINDFUL SPENDING: ALIGNING PURCHASES WITH VALUES

"Too many people spend money they haven't earned, to buy things they don't want, to impress people they don't like."

— Will Rogers

It's simple to fall into the trap of mindless spending in a world where commercialization abounds and we purchase items that don't genuinely enhance our lives. Being frugal with your spending is the secret to creating and preserving wealth, not merely increasing your income or saving a lot of money. Living within your means without compromising the pleasures that really count is the foundation of mindful spending. It involves matching your purchases to your beliefs and eliminating items that are superfluous.

CONSCIOUS CONSUMERISM: SPENDING WITH PURPOSE

To begin spending mindfully, one must first develop consciousness as a consumer. This entails buying with intention as opposed to impulsively or out of habit. Whether it's your family, your health, or your long-term objectives, every dollar you spend should mirror your values.

Is this purchase going to help me achieve my goals? Is it something I really need, or is it just a passing fancy? By asking yourself these questions, you may assess your spending patterns and make sure that your money is being spent on worthwhile endeavors.

For instance, I was tempted to get a fancy car when I started making more money. However, after giving it some serious thinking, I saw that my present vehicle was dependable and took me where I wanted to go. Instead of meeting a real need, the update would have been more about making an impression on others. Thus, I decided to invest that money in my business rather than buy a new car, which ultimately gave me greater financial success and joy.

Considering how your purchases affect the wider community is another aspect of being a conscientious consumer. This could entail avoiding companies that mistreat employees or damage the environment and instead supporting companies that share your beliefs, such as those that emphasize sustainability. Spending with intention makes a positive impact on the world you wish to live in in addition to bettering your own life.

CUTTING UNNECESSARY EXPENSES

One of the easiest ways to align your spending with your values is by cutting out unnecessary expenses. These are the costs that don't add significant value to your life but can add up over time and drain your finances.

Take a hard look at your monthly expenses and ask yourself: do I really need this? Am I getting enough value from this expense to justify the cost? You might be surprised at how many things you're paying for out of habit rather than necessity.

For instance, I once had multiple subscriptions to services I rarely used—magazines, streaming platforms, and a gym membership I never used. By canceling these, I freed up money that I could put towards investments or experiences that brought me more joy.

Another common area where unnecessary expenses pile up is dining out. While it's fine to enjoy a meal at a restaurant now and then, making it a regular habit can take a big bite out of your budget. When I was starting out, I made it a point to cook most of my meals at home. Not only was it cheaper, but it also allowed me to eat healthier and spend more quality time with my family.

Cutting unnecessary expenses doesn't mean depriving yourself of things you enjoy. It's about being intentional with your spending and making sure that your money is going toward things that truly enrich your life. By doing so, you'll find that you have more resources to allocate toward your financial goals, whether that's saving for retirement, investing in your future, or simply enjoying life's simple pleasures.

LIVING BELOW YOUR MEANS WITHOUT SACRIFICING JOY

Living within your means, or spending less than you make, is one of the pillars of financial success. However, many people connect spending less with giving up something or being deprived. It's true that you can live below your means and still enjoy the things you love. It all comes down to setting priorities and realizing that experiences, not material belongings, are what bring true fulfillment.

For instance, I enjoyed basic things like hiking, reading, and having picnics with my family more than I did lavish vacations. In addition to being less expensive, these activities gave me the chance to spend less money while still spending time with my loved ones and appreciating life's beauties.

Resisting the need to keep up with others is another aspect of living below your means. It's simple to get sucked into the comparison trap, particularly in a society where social media is used to promote the positive aspects of people's lives. But keep in mind that real wealth is about being free to live your life as you see fit, not about owning the largest house or the priciest car.

You're not starving yourself when you live within your means; rather, you're giving yourself the gift of financial stability and mental clarity. By doing this, you make sure you have the money to deal with crises, make investments in the future, and follow your passions. Most significantly, though, is that you're releasing yourself from the worry and tension that accompany living paycheck to paycheck.

To sum up, mindful spending involves living within your means without compromising happiness, eliminating needless expenses, and matching your purchases to your ideals. It all comes down to using your money wisely and ensuring that each dollar you spend advances your objectives.

You will not only accumulate wealth by adhering to these ideals, but you will also lead a rich, meaningful life.

CHAPTER 10.
DEBT MANAGEMENT: BREAKING FREE FROM THE CHAINS

"The man who never has money enough to pay his debts has too much of something else."

— James Lendall Basford

You may feel as though debt is a thick chain preventing you from living the life you want. The burden of debt, whether it be from a mortgage, credit card debt, or school debts, may be crippling. But having debt doesn't have to be a permanent thing. You can escape the bonds of debt and maintain your debt-free status for life by using the appropriate techniques.

UNDERSTANDING GOOD VS. BAD DEBT

Not every debt is made equally. The first step to responsibly managing your debt is to recognize the distinctions between good and bad debt.

A healthy debt load is frequently seen as an investment in your future. This includes loans for things like a home mortgage that increases in value, school loans that boost your earning capacity, or loans for a business that helps you make money. If you manage your debt well, good debt can help you accumulate wealth over time.

Bad debt, on the other hand, is money borrowed to finance an unaffordable lifestyle or to buy assets that are losing value. Payday loans, credit card debt with exorbitant interest rates, and auto loans for expensive cars that depreciate the minute you drive them off the lot are examples of this. Unmanageable debt can easily get out of hand, causing stress and restricting your capacity to invest and save money.

I shied away from bad debt like the plague in my early years. I was aware that the interest on every dollar I borrowed for pointless goods would result in substantially higher long-term costs for me. Rather, I concentrated on strategically employing good debt. To launch my first firm, I took out a small loan, and although it was a risk, it paid off by giving me the money I needed to expand.

To effectively manage debt, one must view it as a tool rather than a crutch. If you must take on debt, be sure it is for a purpose that will ultimately enhance your financial status rather than one that would burden you with interest and payment obligations.

STRATEGIES FOR PAYING OFF DEBT QUICKLY

The next step after classifying your debt is to create a strategy to pay it off as soon as you can. The sooner you pay off your debt, the sooner you may start investing your money instead of making interest payments to creditors.

The Debt Snowball Method is among the best methods for debt repayment. This is making minimum payments on your larger bills while paying off your smaller debts first. The money you were contributing to the lowest debt is applied to the next smallest loan, and so on, when the smallest debt has been paid off. Observing debts vanish one by one can provide a tremendous psychological boost.

Another approach is the **Debt Avalanche Method**, where you focus on paying off the debt with the highest interest rate first. This method saves you more money in the long run, as you'll reduce the amount of interest you pay over time. However, it can take longer to see results, which might be less motivating for some people.

Personally, I used a combination of both methods. I started with the Debt Snowball Method to build momentum, paying off small debts that were hanging over my head. Once I gained confidence, I switched to the Debt Avalanche Method to tackle my higher-interest debts. This approach allowed me to stay motivated while also saving money on interest.

It's crucial to think about debt consolidation or refinancing if you can get a better interest rate. By doing this, you can lower your monthly payments and accelerate the repayment of your debt. When combining debt, exercise caution though. You don't want to wind up paying more in the long run by just extending the loan period without lowering the interest rate.

STAYING DEBT-FREE FOR LIFE

Although paying off your debt is a big accomplishment, the journey doesn't stop there. It takes forethought, discipline, and a dedication to live within your means to stay debt-free.

Making and following a budget is one of the best strategies to avoid debt. You can make sure you're not spending more than you make by keeping track of your income and expenses. This lessens the likelihood that you will have to use loans or credit cards to pay for your expenses.

Putting together an emergency fund is also essential. Life will inevitably involve unforeseen costs, and if you don't have a safety net, you risk going back into debt when they do. Try to accumulate enough cash in an accessible account to cover three to six months' worth of living expenditures. Knowing that you can handle problems without taking out a loan can ease your mind.

A crucial next step is to be aware of the inflation of lifestyle. It can be tempting to upgrade your lifestyle when your income rises—buy a bigger house, drive a nicer car, go on more opulent holidays. Enjoying the rewards of your hard work is acceptable, but you shouldn't let your spending spiral out of control and force you to live paycheck to paycheck once more. Recall that real wealth isn't about having a lot of money; it's about being financially free.

And lastly, never waver from your financial objectives. Keeping your objectives in mind will help you avoid giving in to the need to take on needless debt, whether your goal is to invest for the future, save for retirement, or just enjoy living debt-free.

To sum up, managing debt involves recognizing the distinction between good and bad debt, creating a plan to pay off your debts promptly, and making the lifelong commitment to not having any debt. You can liberate yourself from the bonds of debt and create a secure and financially independent life by adhering to these guidelines.

CHAPTER 11. PLANNING FOR THE FUTURE: RETIREMENT AND BEYOND

"The best time to plant a tree was 20 years ago. The second-best time is now."

— Chinese Proverb

It can seem unimportant to plan for the future, particularly when you're preoccupied with accumulating riches or paying for everyday needs. The reality is that your retirement finances and the legacy you leave behind will be significantly impacted by the choices you make today. The good news is that you can ensure future generations benefit from your hard-earned riches and put yourself up for a pleasant retirement even on a low salary with discipline and careful preparation.

RETIREMENT PLANNING ON A LOW INCOME

While it's not feasible for someone living on a little income, retirement can be one of the biggest obstacles. Even if you can just save a tiny amount each month, it's important to start early and stick with it.

Calculating your required retirement income is one of the first steps in retirement planning. Think over your future retirement plans, expected living expenses, existing way of life, and medical costs. Despite the fact that it could seem overwhelming, the power of compound interest allows even modest, regular payments to a retirement account to increase significantly over time.

Make the most of any retirement plan your employer provides, such as a 401(k), especially if they match your contributions. In essence, employer matching is free money, so make a sufficient contribution to receive the entire match. In the event that you are unable to access a 401(k), you should think about forming an IRA. Whereas Roth IRA contributions are paid using after-tax money, traditional IRA contributions offer tax-deferred growth, meaning you won't pay taxes on your earnings until you withdraw them in retirement.

Even with a meager income, I began making contributions to a retirement account in my early years. I'll be honest; it wasn't simple, but I saw those contributions the same as rent or utility payments—they were unavoidable. Those little payments added up over time, and the compound interest effect started to act in my advantage.

THE POWER OF LONG-TERM THINKING

One of the biggest challenges in financial planning is staying committed for the long haul. It's easy to get distracted by short-term wants or discouraged by setbacks. However, long-term thinking is crucial to achieving financial security and success.

It's crucial to fight the urge to take money out of your savings when you're making retirement plans. If you leave your money alone, the money you invest now will grow enormously over time. Not only do you lose the money you took out of your retirement account each time, but you also forfeit any potential growth that money could have made over the years.

Throughout my journey, I have occasionally felt tempted to spend my retirement funds on necessities or wants that arise right away, but I have always forced myself to look beyond that. I was aware that if I maintained my discipline and kept my eyes on the future, my patience would eventually pay off.

Managing your investments is another area where long-term thinking is crucial. Because of this, it's normal to experience anxiety during market downturns. However, historical evidence indicates that markets eventually bounce back and expand. You have a better chance of reaching your financial objectives if you stay the course and avoid taking emotional responses to market turbulence.

LEAVING A LEGACY FOR FUTURE GENERATIONS

Giving your heirs money isn't the only thing that makes a legacy; you also need to convey values, knowledge, and opportunities that will enable them to succeed. Thinking about how you can improve the lives of those you care about is a crucial part of future planning.

Making an estate plan is one approach to leave a lasting legacy. This entails deciding how your assets will be divided upon your passing, making sure that your desires are honored, and providing for your loved ones. For this purpose, a will is a basic but necessary document since it lets you decide who will manage your estate and who will inherit your possessions.

Think about how you might impart your expertise and ideals to the next generation, in addition to leaving a financial legacy. Your children's or grandchildren's life can be significantly impacted by teaching them the value of hard work, saving money, and financial literacy. Not only will kids inherit your wealth, but they will also inherit the values that guided your wealth accumulation.

I understood that I intended to accomplish more with my riches than merely enjoy it while I was still alive when I began to amass it. I wanted to make sure that the community and my family will continue to gain from my achievement for years to come. To handle my assets, I set up a trust and gave precise directions on how my money should be utilized to help future generations. Beyond money, though, I've prioritized imparting the knowledge I've gained so that those who follow in my footsteps can build upon the groundwork I've established.

CHAPTER 12.
LIVING THE MILLIONAIRE LIFESTYLE

"Wealth consists not in having great possessions, but in having few wants."

— **Epictetus**

Accumulating riches alone won't make you a millionaire; you also need to know what it means to be successful in real life. True prosperity, however, goes far beyond flashy vehicles, expansive mansions, and other superficial symbols that many associate with wealth. It's about having the flexibility to live your life as you see fit, security, and freedom. This chapter will discuss how to rethink money, value experiences over material belongings, and use your riches to change the world in a significant way.

REDEFINING WHAT IT MEANS TO BE WEALTHY

What image do you have in mind when you think of a millionaire? Is it someone who drives a fancy car, has a large house, and dresses in designer clothing? Enjoying life's nicer goods is perfectly acceptable, but it's crucial to realize that material possessions don't always translate into actual financial security or happiness.

The ability to make decisions that are consistent with your principles is what defines wealth, not the possessions you hold. It's about being able to go about your life without having to worry about money all the time. This could mean, for some, owning a modest but paid-off house and having the freedom to travel whenever they like. For others, it can mean having the freedom to engage in interests and pastimes without having to worry about finances.

I came to understand that wealth encompassed much more than just having money in the bank during my path to become a millionaire. It was about building a life where I could spend time with my loved ones, follow my hobbies, and give back to my community without ever needing a vacation. To me, true riches is defined as such, and this definition has brought me greater fulfillment than any material acquisition could ever hope to.

EXPERIENCES OVER POSSESSIONS: FINDING TRUE HAPPINESS

Among the most important things I've ever learned is that experiences make you happier than material stuff by a wide margin. A new car or the newest technology may provide a short-term rush, but experiences like traveling, spending time with loved ones, and learning new things are what make lifelong memories and bring true joy.

This theory is supported by research, which indicates that those who prioritize experiences above possessions are typically happy over time. This is due to the fact that happiness is derived from experiences in three stages: anticipation, the actual event, and the memories that follow. On the other side, possessions often become dull rapidly.

When I was able to buy more luxuries, I started to wonder if having these things would really make my life better. I opted, more often than not, to spend my money on experiences. I experienced new things, saw new locations, and created lifelong memories. My life has been enhanced by these events in a manner that a fancy automobile or clothing could never match.

Experiences also seem to strengthen bonds between people, in my observation. Bonds that material possessions just cannot replace are formed through activities like eating dinner together, traveling to a new city with friends, or learning a new skill with a spouse. These relationships are ultimately what lead to actual happiness.

GIVING BACK: USING WEALTH FOR GOOD

Being able to give back is one of the most satisfying parts of becoming rich. Using your wealth for good is a potent way to make a lasting influence, whether it's by investing in your community, supporting organizations you care about, or giving to those in need.

Giving back has always been important to me. I consider it my duty to use my financial success—which I have been fortunate enough to attain—to benefit others. This implies that you don't need to be a multibillionaire philanthropist to change the world. Generosity, even in little doses, may make a big difference.

Donating can take many different shapes. It could be giving to charitable organizations, giving of your time, or even serving as a mentor to someone who is just starting out in their profession.

Finding methods to use your resources to improve the world is what matters most.

Giving back, in addition, gives me a sense of contentment and purpose that money cannot buy. One of the most fulfilling elements of money is knowing that you've improved someone else's life, supported a cause you care about, or contributed to the prosperity of your town.

CHAPTER 13. BECOMING FINANCIALLY INDEPENDENT

"Financial independence is the ability to live from the income of your own personal resources."

— Jim Rohn

Reaching financial independence is the ultimate aim on the path to riches, not merely a goal in and of itself. It's the moment when you can live life on your terms, when you no longer need a job to make ends meet, and when your money starts working for you. The actions you must take to become financially independent, the mentality that will direct you, and the significance of acknowledging your accomplishments and sharing your path with others are all covered in this chapter.

ACHIEVING FINANCIAL INDEPENDENCE AND FREEDOM

Having enough assets to support your living needs without having to work for a wage is what it means to be financially independent. It's about putting in place a safety net so you may explore new chances, spend time with loved ones, and follow your passions without worrying about money.

The first step in achieving financial independence is realizing that managing, saving, and investing your money are equally as important as having a large income. If you're not handling your money well, you can be financially reliant even when you make a lot of money. On the other hand, if you manage your money wisely and with discipline, you can be financially independent even with a little salary.

Living below your means is a crucial step towards reaching financial independence. This entails being conscious of your spending and ensuring that your outlays are in line with your long-term objectives, but it also doesn't entail denying yourself of everything you like. Your time to financial freedom will increase with the amount you can invest and save.

It's also vital to concentrate on developing several revenue sources. This may be accomplished through investments, side projects, or passive revenue streams like dividends or rental properties. To avoid depending entirely on one source of income, it's important to diversify your sources.

THE STEPS TO BECOMING A SELF-MADE MILLIONAIRE

Becoming a self-made millionaire requires a combination of discipline, determination, and smart financial decisions. Here are the key steps to guide you on this journey:

1. Set Clear Financial Goals: Establish your own definition of financial independence first. What is the necessary amount of money to live well in retirement? What kind of way of life are you looking for? Establishing measurable, precise goals can help you stay focused and provide you with something to aim for.

2. Create a Solid Financial Plan: A budget, a savings plan, and an investing strategy should all be part of your financial plan. Ensure that your plan is reasonable and appropriate for your level of income and way of life. To stay on course, check your plan frequently and make necessary adjustments.

3. Maximize Your Income: Seek opportunities to boost your income by launching your own company, doing side gigs, or receiving promotions. Your ability to save and invest increases with income.

4. Invest Wisely: One of the most effective methods for accumulating wealth is investing. Put your attention on long-term investments with room for growth, like mutual funds, equities, and real estate. To lower risk, make sure your investments are diversified.

5. Minimize Debt: One of the biggest barriers to financial independence might be debt. Make paying off high-interest debt your top priority, and try to avoid taking on additional debt at all costs. If you must borrow money, make sure it's for a home or an education—things that will appreciate in value.

6. Live Below Your Means: This is a concept that keeps coming up because it's so crucial. You may save and invest more money if you spend less. Look for ways to reduce wasteful spending and concentrate on allocating funds for the things that are most important to you.

7. Stay Disciplined: Financial freedom requires work and patience to achieve. Hold fast to your objectives, even in the face of difficulty. Keep your focus on the goal and never forget why you embarked on this path.

8. Continue Learning: It's critical to continue studying because the financial world is always evolving. Learn new financial techniques and trends by reading books, attending classes, and keeping up with current events. The more information you possess, the more capable you will be of making wise financial choices.

CELEBRATING YOUR SUCCESS AND SHARING YOUR STORY

Being financially independent is a noteworthy accomplishment that should be honored. It is the result of years of diligence, self-control, and astute judgment. It's also a chance for you to consider the lessons you've learned and the ways in which you may apply your knowledge to benefit others.

Although you've earned it, you don't have to spend a lot of money to celebrate your achievement. It's still okay to treat yourself. It could be as easy as pausing to recognize your progress and the freedom that comes with being financially independent. To stay motivated and keep increasing your wealth, you might also want to set fresh objectives for yourself.

Another method to commemorate your achievement is to tell your tale. You may encourage and inform individuals who are just beginning on their own path to financial freedom by sharing your story with others. Telling your story, whether by writing, speaking, or mentoring, has the capacity to transform lives.

To be financially independent is to be truly free. It's about being in charge of your time, your decisions, and your destiny. You can have that freedom and design the kind of life you really love by implementing the strategies described in this chapter. And when you do, remember to enjoy your accomplishments and tell the world about your experience—you deserve it.

CONCLUSION: YOUR PATH TO WEALTH

It's crucial that you pause as you near the finish of this book and consider your journey. Consider your starting point, your learnings, and your progress. You've made the time to invest in yourself and establish a solid knowledge base that will sustain your future financial development. That's no easy task.

Building wealth involves more than just saving money. It all comes down to cultivating the proper attitude, choosing wisely, and persevering through difficult times. It's about appreciating your accomplishments, growing from your mistakes, and never giving up. Just by committing to your financial future and searching out this information, you have already made great progress.

Recall that each little step you take counts as a step forward. Every action you take toward financial independence, whether it's increasing your monthly savings, making your first investment, or just altering your mindset, will get you one step closer to your goal. Take stock of your current accomplishments and feel proud of your growth.

THE ONGOING PURSUIT OF GROWTH AND KNOWLEDGE

This is not the end of the road to riches. Actually, it's only getting started. Achieving financial success is a continual process that calls for constant learning and development. You should always be changing along with the financial world.

Maintain your curiosity. Whether it's through books, podcasts, or guidance from others who have been there before you, never stop learning new things. You'll be better able to handle the chances and challenges that lie ahead the more knowledge you acquire. Keep in mind that wealth is more than just money; it's also about information, experiences, and the discernment to make choices that are consistent with your objectives and ideals.

Never hesitate to modify your tactics as you go. Your goals may change more as you develop. It's alright. Adaptability and flexibility are essential characteristics of successful people. While keeping your sights set on the goal, remain receptive to the various routes that could lead you there.

FINAL WORDS OF ENCOURAGEMENT

I want to give you a few last words of encouragement before we part ways. By dedicating yourself to your financial education, you've made a significant progress—something that many individuals never accomplish. You should be proud of the way you've distinguished yourself.

Recall that acquiring wealth is a process rather than a destination. It's about taking little steps toward improvement each and every day. It all comes down to maintaining focus on your objectives and refusing to let failure demoralize you. You already possess all the qualities you need to succeed, including perseverance, tenacity, and the knowledge this book has given you.

Since we're talking about the journey, how about we assist others in discovering their own route to financial success? I would appreciate it if you could take a time to write a review if you thought this book was worthwhile. More people may learn about these techniques and go on their own paths to financial independence with the assistance of your comments. Furthermore, who knows? Someone else could use your evaluation as motivation to take the initial step.

I appreciate you traveling with me on this trip. Continue learning, keep moving forward, and most importantly, never stop believing in yourself. Although achieving riches is not always simple, it is completely possible if you have the correct attitude and resources. Cheers to your triumph and the amazing future you're creating!

BIBLIOGRAPHY

1. **Kiyosaki, Robert T.** Rich Dad Poor Dad: What the Rich Teach Their Kids About Money That the Poor and Middle Class Do Not! Plata Publishing, 1997.

2. **Eker, T. Harv.** Secrets of the Millionaire Mind: Mastering the Inner Game of Wealth. HarperBusiness, 2005.

3. **Ramsey, Dave.** The Total Money Makeover: A Proven Plan for Financial Fitness. Thomas Nelson, 2003.

4. **Orman, Suze.** The Money Book for the Young, Fabulous & Broke. Riverhead Books, 2005.

5. **Mandelbrot, Benoit, and Richard L. Hudson.** The (Mis)Behavior of Markets: A Fractal View of Risk, Ruin, and Reward. Basic Books, 2004.

6. **Ferriss, Timothy.** The 4-Hour Workweek: Escape 9-5, Live Anywhere, and Join the New Rich. Crown Publishers, 2007.

7. **Vanderkam, Laura.** All the Money in the World: What the Happiest People Know About Getting and Spending. Portfolio, 2012.

8. **Collins, James C., and Jerry I. Porras.** Built to Last: Successful Habits of Visionary Companies. HarperBusiness, 1994.

9. **Sethi, Ramit.** I Will Teach You to Be Rich. Workman Publishing, 2009.

10. **Hill, Napoleon.** Think and Grow Rich. The Ralston Society, 1937.

11. **Stanley, Thomas J., and William D. Danko.** The Millionaire Next Door: The Surprising Secrets of America's Wealthy. Longstreet Press, 1996.

12. **Schwab, Charles R.** Charles Schwab's Guide to Financial Independence: Simple Solutions for Busy People. Crown Business, 1998.

13. **Buffett, Warren, and Lawrence A. Cunningham.** The Essays of Warren Buffett: Lessons for Corporate America. The Cunningham Group, 1997.

14. **Bogle, John C.** The Little Book of Common Sense Investing: The Only Way to Guarantee Your Fair Share of Stock Market Returns.* Wiley, 2007.

15. **Grant, Adam.** Give and Take: Why Helping Others Drives Our Success. Viking, 2013.

www.ingramcontent.com/pod-product-compliance
Lightning Source LLC
Chambersburg PA
CBHW050309230526
45471CB00005B/2090